DOGS AND CATS

Remedies Straight from Your Kitchen

GERALD T. EDISON

AuthorHouse™
1663 Liberty Drive
Bloomington, IN 47403
www.authorhouse.com
Phone: 833-262-8899

Because of the dynamic nature of the Internet, any web addresses or links contained in this book may have changed since publication and may no longer be valid. The views expressed in this work are solely those of the author and do not necessarily reflect the views of the publisher, and the publisher hereby disclaims any responsibility for them.

Any people depicted in stock imagery provided by Getty Images are models, and such images are being used for illustrative purposes only. Certain stock imagery © Getty Images.

This book is printed on acid-free paper.

ISBN: 978-1-4567-3627-9 (sc)
ISBN: 978-1-4817-2712-9 (e)

Print information available on the last page.

Published by AuthorHouse 03/08/2021

authorHOUSE®

Contents

Introduction

In this economy we're living in today, everything is high-priced and you get little for your money. Prices are continually rising for daily necessities, such as health insurance, gas and maintenance for automobiles, food for the household, telephones, cable, lights, gas, and, for many people, prescription medicine. Yet, somehow, the wages we make on our jobs stay the same. Even the cost of taking care of our pets has skyrocketed. But there are some things that won't cost you an arm and a leg for your pets.

For twenty-seven years I ran my own kennel, and I used home remedies for my pets. I used household supplies straight out of the kitchen to heal the dogs, and by doing so, I saved lots of money that otherwise would have been spent on trips to the veterinarian.

This book is short and simple, and it shows you how you can save your dog's or cat's life right from the kitchen, by using everyday things we pick up from the grocery store. And the best part is, these remedies are all natural.

Catching and Curing Parvovirus in Time

Parvovirus can be cured if caught in time, but you have to recognize early symptoms in your pets. The following are some of the symptoms of parvovirus:

→ Walking slowly

→ Not drinking water

→ Lying around

→ Very foul smell from the stool

→ Vomiting liquids from the mouth

→ Diarrhea

→ Weight loss

→ Blood coming from the back end

→ Sleeping all day

Instructions:

If you see some of these signs in your dog or cat, this is a remedy you can use: Fry three or four slices of bacon and save the grease with all the bacon crumbs in it. Wait until the bacon grease cools and then feed the grease to your pet. If the animal can't eat it on its own, open its mouth and force the grease down its throat the best you can, and then rub the throat with your hand so your pet can swallow. If the animal vomits the grease up, give it to him/her again and again until it stays down. The following are approximate grease dosages:

→ One teaspoon for cats and small dogs

→ One big, wide-mouthed spoon for large dogs

After your pet holds down the bacon grease, one other ingredient goes with it: Pedialyte. The same electrolyte solution used for children can be use for your pets; it will boost your dog or cat back up and will help replenish the fluids lost from the sickness.

If the grease and Pedialyte stay in your pet's stomach, your pet will likely live.

Instructions:

You will need a small eye-drop bottle. If you do not have an eye-drop bottle, you may substitute any squeeze bottle you have.

Rinse out the bottle with hot water and then punch a bigger hole in the bottle's opening. Put Pedialyte in the bottle and hold your pet's head back. Open your pet's mouth and squeeze out the liquid. Make sure the animal swallows, and then you're done. The more Pedialyte you get in its mouth, the quicker your pet will recover.

If parvovirus is caught in time, this remedy can save your pet. I know it doesn't sound like much, but it works.

In dealing with pets, always keep bacon grease stored on the countertop or in the refrigerator; it can be useful for your pet. Use the bacon grease once a month. It won't hurt them, but get ready for the stool coming out the back end.

Bacon grease can also be used for the following:

→ Swollen paws
→ Swollen legs
→ Cleaning your pet's digestive system
→ Swollen gums

Worming Your Dog or Cat

When it comes to worming your pets, there is a very simple and safe method that can keep your pets healthy through their lives: pure garlic. Garlic takes care of many afflictions in your pets' bodies.

Pure garlic takes care of the following parasites:

- → Worms
- → Ticks
- → Fleas
- → Mosquitoes
- → Tapeworms
- → Roundworms
- → Ringworms
- → Whipworms

Instructions:

Cut off a little piece of garlic, put it in some meat or in another food your pet likes, and then feed it to your pet. If the animal won't eat, you can get garlic pills from a health-food store.

For puppies, you should administer garlic every two weeks for three months. For grown dogs, you should use garlic once a month. It is good for them because it is all natural.

NOTE: Outside dogs have stronger appetites than in-house dogs.

If you feed your pet pure garlic as described, you will see a difference in your pet's attitude.

Cleaning Pets' Ears and Wounds

Your pet's ears can be cleaned with peroxide and medicated Vaseline, and olive oil can be used for earaches—again, these are common household items. (However, you may have to go online to find the medicated Vaseline, depending on your location, if you do not have it handy.) These substances are good for the following:

→ Sores

→ Cuts

→ Earaches

Instructions:

Pour ¼ of peroxide into a cup and then dip gauze into the peroxide. Ring out the excess liquid and then use the gauze to clean your pet's ears. If there are sores in the ears, follow the peroxide application with mediated Vaseline. Rub the Vaseline on your fingers and use your fingers to put it in the animal's ears. Not a lot of Vaseline is required.

NOTE: If your dog or cat keeps shaking its head constantly and moaning, it probably has an earache.

If your pet has an earache, olive oil can be used to stop the aches.

Instructions:

You can use an eye-drop bottle to administer the olive oil. Warm up olive oil on a wide-mouthed spoon or in a small pot. Test the temperature of the oil on your skin first, to make sure it's warm, and then put two drops of the oil in each of your pet's ears. Once the drops are in the ears, you're done. You should only use this remedy when needed.

Joint Relief for Your Pet in Old Age

Here's a remedy you can use on your pets while they're young in order to help them in their old age: cod liver oil. Cod liver oil can help your pet to maintain all of the following:

→ A healthy digestive tract

→ Strong bones

→ Strong teeth

→ An attractive coat

→ Joint relief

→ Relief from aches

→ Pain relief

Instructions:

For small dogs and cats, give your pet one teaspoon of cod liver oil mixed with food once a week.

For large dogs, give two tablespoons of cod liver oil once a week.

NOTE: I found it easier to put the cod liver oil in a can of meat my dogs liked, but if all else fails, capsules are available at health-foods store and supermarkets.

Growing Back Pets' Lost Hair

Many dogs or cats can lose their hair from sickness or even just from fighting. These common items are a remedy for hair loss:

→ Dirty motor oil
→ Brewer's yeast

Instructions:

Take dirty motor oil, rub it in your hands, and then put it on your pet. Rub the oil wherever the hair loss has occurred. Two weeks later, wash off the oil really well with dish washing liquid. (Dawn works well.)

NOTE: You can get dirty motor oil from your closest junkyard, and brewer's yeast can be found at health-food stores.

WARNINGS:

Do not rub motor oil on an outdoor pet in winter weather.
Oil will mess up your house; for inside dogs, use brewer's yeast.

Curing Pets' Colds

If your pet has a runny nose, mucus coming out of its mouth, and cold in its eyes, it probably has a cold. The following remedy can be used (though I only used this one on in-house animals): Vicks VapoRub topical ointment.

Instructions:

Rub Vicks VapoRub on the upper and lower chest of your pet and then fold and pin a towel tight on the animal's chest. If the towel doesn't stay in place, put a walking harness on your pet to hold the towel up.

Your pet can generally heal in a day or two.

NOTE: Make sure to clean mucus up overnight. You can use a syringe if necessary for mucus in the nose.

Vitamin E

Here's a remedy for your stud dog, if needed, to aid in breeding: vitamin E (100 IU).

Instructions:

Give your pet one capsule a week for two weeks, just before breeding.

NOTE: Only use as necessary for your pet.

This concludes a few dog and cat remedies, straight out of the kitchen, that I used for twenty-seven years. Don't be afraid to use them, because they're all natural.

Printed in the United States
by Baker & Taylor Publisher Services